HOW TO BUY AND SELL ON EBAY WITHOUT GETTING SCREWED

FRAZIER CUNNINGHAM III

Copyright © 2021 FRAZIER CUNNINGHAM III

All rights reserved

The characters and events portrayed in this book are fictitious. Any similarity to real persons, living or dead, is coincidental and not intended by the author.

No part of this book may be reproduced, or stored in a retrieval system, or transmitted in any form or by any means, electronic, mechanical, photocopying, recording, or otherwise, without express written permission of the publisher.

ISBN-13: 9798758357262
ISBN-10: 1477123456

Cover design by: Frazier Cunningham
Library of Congress Control Number: 2018675309
Printed in the United States of America

CONTENTS

Title Page
Copyright
Introduction | 1
Where Do I Start? | 3
What Do I Sell? | 6
How Do I Price My Items? | 12
Navigating New Seller Restrictions on ebay | 15
Auction Or Buy It Now? | 18
How Much Does It Cost To List My Items? | 21
How To Craft An Effective Ebay Listing | 24
Mastering The Art Of Shipping ON Ebay: A Comprehensive Guide | 29
Navigating the Complexities of Getting Paid On Ebay | 32
The Ultimate Guide to Customer Service on eBay | 35
The eBay Buyer's Bible: Everything You Need to Know to Buy Smart and Save Money | 38
Taking Flight: Your eBay Journey Ahead | 43
About The Author | 47

INTRODUCTION

Let's start this off with a confession – I have a love/hate relationship with eBay. I mean, I hate eBay as a corporation with a passion! If eBay was a person I would have "slapped the taste" out of its mouth already. I mean, I would really, really, like to fight eBay in the streets.

On the other hand, I love eBay for giving me the platform to run a successful home business. Without eBay my wife and I would never have been able to have the reach and the audience we do without any startup capital. Over the years I have created multiple million-dollar companies using the eBay platform.

With that being said, eBay is a righteous pain in the behind to deal with. They are constantly changing the rules and rug pulling me. The agents are no more knowledgeable than the customers and rarely, if ever, do their job competently. That is why I decided to write this book. I have learned over the decades how to work the eBay system. Sure, I am constantly learning because eBay is constantly "evolving" but for the most part I have it down packed. Where others have tried and given up, I have flourished so it is my joy to be able to share my knowledge with others.

So, now that we have that little bit out of the way let's get started.

Hello, my name is Frazier and I am an eBayaholic. Even though eBay has been the source of much stress in my life I keep coming back to it. It's an addiction. Perhaps I could stop but I really don't want to. It's just too good to me. It's been 20 years now since I became an eBay seller. It started simply enough, with me selling things I no longer needed. This was back in the days when eBay was still an online swap meet. It was a much simpler time. But even then, eBay had impossible rules that changed with the wind. It was like navigating a minefield while blindfolded and drunk. I have received numerous lifetime bans, from both eBay and PayPal, I have had my feedback decimated and my online reputation ruined....But, I learned from all of that. Now I maintain a 100% feedback rate despite buyers having a chronic case of buyer's remorse, I have multiple healthy eBay accounts and a thriving business. And no, I will not be disclosing my eBay accounts in this book. People are petty, I'm sure that you aren't one of those people, but I was once told "duct tape is grey and silence is golden", so for that reason all the stories in this book will be based on true stories but something will be changed to protect the innocent.

What I will do is walk you through the process of setting up your eBay account for success, show you how to deliver good customer service without having to bend over and take it up the rear, and finally, how to deal with eBay customer service so you can get your way every time.

WHERE DO I START?

Embarking on an eBay journey as a novice can feel like a tightrope walk with the ground nowhere in sight. The secret is, the challenges are part of the process. To overcome them, you just have to be a step ahead. Here's a road map to guide you through setting up your eBay business successfully.

Choose A Memorable Username And Profile Picture

First impressions are virtual but they can make or break your business. Your username is the first thing that potential buyers see. Think of something catchy yet professional. Avoid generic usernames like 'momof4' or 'entrepreneur4life'. These may describe you, but they don't set you apart from the millions of other users on eBay. Aim for a name that is unique, easy to remember, and preferably resonates with the niche you choose. If you're selling vintage watches, how about 'TimelessTreasures201'? Your profile picture should also align with your brand; it should be clean, professional, and relevant to what you're selling.

Identify Your Niche

The phrase 'Jack of all trades, master of none' could not be more accurate when it comes to eBay selling. Focus is key. While it may be tempting to sell anything and everything, a well-defined niche allows you to target your marketing and inventory more effectively. If you have a passion for skincare, dive into that world. Become an expert in it. Source quality skincare goods and focus your effort on selling those. Alternatively, if you are keen on the thrift store model, make sure you're offering something unique or specialized, such as vintage clothing or rare books. Understanding your niche can also help you figure out the right pricing strategy, the best way to list your items, and how to connect with specific customer needs.

Consider If You Need A Storefront

An eBay Store subscription comes with its own set of benefits—like more free listings per month and lower final value fees—but it also comes with a monthly cost. If you're just dipping your toes in the water, hold off on committing to a subscription. You can start by selling items without a store, and you can still list plenty of items and get a feel for the business. Once you see consistent sales, and you are ready to ramp up marketing efforts such as issuing coupons or creating seasonal promotions, then it would make sense to consider opening an eBay Store.

Financial Planning

Before you get lost in the eBay vortex, set a budget for yourself. Consider the initial investments you'll need for inventory, shipping supplies, and other operational costs. Keep tabs on your revenue and expenses. You don't need a sophisticated accounting system when you're starting, but a simple Excel sheet tracking your money in and out can make a world of difference. This will also help you evaluate when it's the right time to perhaps expand or open an eBay store, as mentioned earlier.

Know Your Policies

Before you get lost in the eBay vortex, set a budget for yourself. Consider the initial investments you'll need for inventory, shipping supplies, and other operational costs. Keep tabs on your revenue and expenses. You don't need a sophisticated accounting system when you're starting, but a simple Excel sheet tracking your money in and out can make a world of difference. This will also help you evaluate when it's the right time to perhaps expand or open an eBay store, as mentioned earlier.

Build Trust With Customer Service

Lastly but crucially, always remember that trust is currency in any business, more so online. Ship items promptly, describe listings accurately, respond to queries timely, and address issues professionally. A good reputation will earn you positive reviews and repeat customers, which are invaluable.

Starting an eBay business doesn't have to be daunting if you equip yourself with the right tools and information. Happy selling!

WHAT DO I SELL?

The first hurdle you face when starting your eBay business is identifying what to sell. With an overwhelming number of options, it's easy to get lost or paralyzed by choices. However, it's simpler than you think. In this chapter, we will explore three main avenues for sourcing products: reselling used goods, buying low to sell high, and dropshipping.

Option One: Resell Used Goods

The Hidden Treasures in Your Home

Surprisingly, your home is a treasure trove of items you can sell. Think about that drawer full of cords that have accumulated over the years. It's not junk; it's inventory. Here's how to unearth the sellable items in your home:

1. **Go Room by Room**: Make an inventory of items you no longer need or use.
2. **Assess Condition**: Some items may need minor repairs or cleaning.
3. **Market Research**: Check eBay to see what similar items are selling for.

Potential Items to Consider
- Empty printer cartridges
- Unused school supplies

- Unwanted clothing
- Craft supplies (popsicle sticks, toilet paper rolls, paper towel rolls, etc.)
- Broken items (sold for parts)
- Anything new in the package

Benefits
- Minimal initial investment
- Environmentally friendly
- Convenient and easy to start

Option Two: Buy Low, Sell High

Research and Source Products

The principle here is simple: buy cheap, sell high. However, you need to do market research to find these opportunities. Tools like eBay's "Completed Listings" can help you identify items with high profit potential. Let me illustrate this with a true story:

> Imagine my surprise when I discovered that standing mirrors, those unassuming household items, were in unexpectedly high demand on eBay. Why, you ask? I haven't the foggiest. But this revelation came about in an almost serendipitous fashion. My daughter, ever keen on her appearance, expressed her desire for a full-length standing mirror to "check the fit," as she endearingly phrased it. I naively thought procuring such an item online would be both economical and convenient. How wrong I was!
>
> As it turned out, I found the mirror she wanted not on Amazon or eBay, but at our neighborhood Walmart—$45 cheaper, no less! The very same mirror I'd seen listed on eBay for $135 plus $10 shipping was right there, practically gift-wrapped for me at $90.

That's when my internal money-making radar sprang to life, like a divining rod sensing water beneath parched earth. Here was an opportunity, staring me right in the face, requiring almost zero investment upfront. So, I jumped in.

Using Walmart's stock photos and product descriptions, I created an eBay listing for these sought-after mirrors. I marked them at a competitive $126 with an additional $10 for shipping, and set my quantity at 10. Then I waited, with bated breath and crossed fingers.

Lo and behold, the mirrors started selling. Each time the eBay notification chimed on my phone, I'd scurry down to Walmart, buy another mirror, slap a shipping label on it, and hand it over to the ever-reliable UPS for delivery.

So, there it was—a simple, risk-free enterprise, born out of a casual shopping trip and a discerning eye for opportunity. And let this tale serve as a lesson that sometimes, the most lucrative opportunities are hiding in plain sight, just waiting for someone to seize them.

Where To Source Inventory

- Thrift stores: Designer handbags, trendy clothing, jewelry, and more
- Outlet stores: Think BigLots or Ollies
- Clearance aisles: Discounted goods in mainstream stores
- Local dry cleaners: Unclaimed items
- Garage, yard, and estate sales
- Online marketplaces: Craigslist, Offerup, Letgo

Benefits

- Wider range of inventory
- Higher potential profits

- Opportunity to specialize in a niche

Option Three: Dropshipping

How Does It Work?
You list a product on eBay that you don't physically have. When it sells, you order it from a third-party supplier who ships it directly to the customer.

Pros and Cons

Pros:
- Low risk
- No need for storage space

Cons:
- Lower profit margins
- Less control over stock and shipping
- eBay restrictions on dropshipping

Reliable Dropshipping Platforms

Wholesale2B - Wholesale2B offers more than 1 million products ready to be drop shipped. on top of that, they allow you to sell products on: eBay, Amazon, WooCommerce, Shopify, Magento, Weebly, BigCommerce, your own Wholesale2B store (handle the orders yourself by becoming a registered reseller with each supplier or pay Wholesale2B a 3% fee to handle that for you). Wholesale2B starts free and includes their 1 million products, customer support, and a lifetime free account.

Saleshoo - Saleshoo is a great dropshipper that offers a massive supplier database to draw on. A $67 yearly membership with

Salehoo grants you access to this database of 8,000+ wholesalers and dropshippers.
They're all screened by SaleHoo before they're added to the directory. There's a 60-day free trial period

Spocket - Spocket gives you a great database app of dropshipping items. They make it easy to find US and EU items that'll ship within your country rather than from China, cutting down on slow ship speeds. The Basic plan (25 products with unlimited orders) is free, and upgrading to Pro is $49 per month for 250 products and branded invoicing. The Empire plan unlocks unlimited products for $99 per month.

Worldwide Brands - For $299, you can get a lifetime subscription to Worldwide Brand's database of wholesalers and dropshippers. It's a great budget-friendly solution for those competing to sell products on Amazon, eBay, and Etsy. Worldwide Brands distinguishes itself with its extensive upper-market wholesale directory of certified drop shippers and its reliable and quick-to-respond support team. The lifetime membership certainly doesn't hurt either.

Sellvia - Sellvia is $39 per month or $299 per year but offers a free month trial. Trust me, it is worth giving Sellvia a shot. It is an ecommerce supplier with its own fulfillment center located in California, US. Sellvia is focused on addressing the biggest pain point of drop shippers, which is long shipping times to the US. is processed by its team within 24 hours and shipped to the customer within 1-3 business days.

Tips for Success
- Choose reliable suppliers
- Keep an eye on inventory levels
- Ensure fast shipping times

Allowed And Prohibited Items

You also have to consider eBay's rules and regulations. Violating these rules could get your account limited or banned. Here are some general guidelines:

Do Not List:
- Drugs, alcohol, counterfeit items, stolen goods
- Items using copyrighted images from other websites

eBay Best Practices:

- Always complete sales within the eBay platform
- Avoid canceling customer orders
- Address buyer complaints promptly
- Provide accurate and detailed listings

Whether you choose to resell items from your home, buy low to sell high, or engage in dropshipping, success comes from research, dedication, and compliance with eBay's rules. Each method has its pros and cons, so choose the one that aligns best with your goals, skills, and resources. Happy selling!

HOW DO I PRICE MY ITEMS?

Properly pricing your items on eBay can mean the difference between making a sale and having your item gather digital dust on the virtual shelves. The price tag you put on your goods should be determined after careful research and consideration. But before you set your price, it's crucial to understand the unique market dynamics on eBay, which can vary dramatically from traditional retail settings.

Manual Research: A Step-By-Step Guide

Step 1: Conduct a Search for Your Item

Start by entering the name of your item into the eBay search bar. Be as specific as possible to narrow down the results. For instance, if you're selling scrapbooking paper with stickers, type "Scrapbooking paper with stickers."

Step 2: Filter to See Sold Items

On the left-hand side of the desktop version or the upper right-hand corner of the mobile version, you'll find a filter option. Select "Sold Items" from the list. This will display a list of similar items that have already been sold on eBay, giving you an idea of the demand for your item.

Step 3: Sort from Highest to Lowest Price

Use the "Sort" function, usually located at the top of the page, to sort the items from highest to lowest price, including shipping costs. This will give you an idea of the highest price that buyers are willing to pay for a similar item.

After performing these steps, you'll have a rough idea of how to competitively price your item based on current market rates.

Using Terapeak Product Research

For those who prefer a more automated and analytical approach, eBay offers a tool called Terapeak Product Research. Found under the "Research" tab in the Seller Hub, this tool is free for all sellers.

Features of Terapeak Product Research:
- Comprehensive Reports: Terapeak gathers sales data and presents it in a simple line graph, making it easier to understand market trends.
- Optimization Tips: The tool provides hints on how you can optimize your listings by showing you successful strategies employed by other sellers, like shipping policies and item specifics.

Advanced Tools for eBay Store Owners: Terapeak Sourcing Insights

If you own an eBay store, you gain access to an additional tool known as Terapeak Sourcing Insights. This feature provides advanced functionalities that can substantially enhance your sales strategy.

What Terapeak Sourcing Insights Offers:

- **High Demand, Low Supply Identification**: It helps you pinpoint categories where demand is high but supply is low, giving you the chance to capitalize on these opportunities.
- **Trend Analysis Over Time**: By showing trends over various periods, you can stay ahead of seasonal demands and adapt your inventory accordingly.
- **Sales Data Utilization**: Using this real-time sales data, you can refresh your inventory based on current buyer preferences.

Whether you opt for manual research or use eBay's advanced tools, understanding how to price your items is a crucial aspect of being a successful seller. Remember, setting the right price isn't just about maximizing your profits; it's also about providing value to your customers. By combining your insights from manual research with the data provided by Terapeak tools, you'll be well-equipped to price your items effectively and competitively.

NAVIGATING NEW SELLER RESTRICTIONS ON EBAY

If you're a newcomer to the world of eBay selling, it's essential to know that the platform enforces certain restrictions to protect buyers and ensure a quality marketplace. As a new seller, you'll find that your ability to list items is restricted both in quantity and value. This continues until you earn a feedback score of at least 10. Even after reaching this milestone, you'll encounter some remaining limitations.

The Myth of 'Buying' Feedback

You may come across advice suggesting you can "buy" your way to a higher feedback score by engaging in transactions involving low-cost items, such as $1 trinkets. While this may seem like an easy way to bolster your profile, be warned: eBay is aware of this tactic, and it could put your seller standing at risk.

Selling Useful but Digital Goods

Instead of trying to game the system, consider offering something valuable yet easily transferable. One strategy I've found effective is buying UPC codes in bulk for around $20, and then reselling them. Digital goods like these don't require shipping and are in frequent demand, making them an excellent choice for new sellers looking to build their profiles.

Importance of Feedback

In your product listings, emphasize the importance of feedback. Mention that you're willing to reciprocate with positive feedback for the buyer. This creates a win-win scenario, as both parties are interested in enhancing their eBay reputation. It's essential to make these initial feedbacks count, as they will set the tone for your future transactions.

Leveraging Feedback to Create Trust

The aim is not just to bypass eBay's initial limitations—although that's certainly a benefit—but also to instill confidence among potential buyers. A strong feedback score provides a sense of reliability, encouraging users to take a chance on a new seller.

Other Limitations: The 90-Day Rule on Bulk Listing Tools

As a new seller, you're prohibited from using eBay's bulk listing tools for the first 90 days after your first sale. This might seem like an inconvenience, but these tools are mainly useful for sellers managing thousands of listings, so it's not a significant hindrance when you're just starting out.

Why These Restrictions Exist

Though these restrictions may feel like unnecessary hurdles, they serve a crucial purpose: they protect buyers from fraud and ensure that new sellers understand the platform's nuances before diving in. These safeguards help maintain eBay's reputation as a trustworthy marketplace.

The Road Ahead

Even as you gain experience and build up your seller profile, don't be surprised if you encounter further restrictions or challenges. eBay is an evolving platform with rules that can change based on various factors, including seller performance and marketplace trends. But the better your understanding of these initial limitations, the smoother your transition to becoming a seasoned eBay seller will be.

AUCTION OR BUY IT NOW?
Navigating eBay's Selling Formats

The landscape of eBay has evolved tremendously since its inception as an online marketplace primarily based on auctions. These days, a majority of items are sold through the "Buy It Now" format, but that doesn't mean auctions have become obsolete. Both methods have their pros and cons, depending on the type of item you're selling, the demand for it, and other market factors. In this chapter, we'll delve into the intricacies of both formats to help you make an informed decision on which one is best suited for you.

The Allure Of Auctions: Scarcity And Demand

Auctions are exciting for both buyers and sellers. For sellers, the primary advantage comes when the product you're offering is in high demand and low supply. Imagine having access to a pre-release PlayStation 6 (or whatever version they're up to now). If it's the holiday season, you're looking at an optimal setting for a bidding war.

In such a scenario, auctions can be your best friend. The

excitement and competition of a live auction often drive the prices higher than the market value. For highly coveted items, the auction format may allow you to pocket more than you'd get through a fixed price.

The Other Side Of The Coin: When Auctions Aren't Ideal

The auction format is not always your best bet. Consider attempting to sell a PlayStation 1 in February, when many buyers are financially recovering from the holiday season. Auctions depend on active participation, and if there aren't enough interested buyers, your item may sell for less than its worth or, worse, not sell at all.

Also, auctions have a maximum duration of 10 days and have to be manually relisted if the item doesn't sell, adding more work for the seller.

The Perks Of "Buy It Now"

While auctions can be volatile, the "Buy It Now" option provides a more stable and controlled selling environment. Here are some benefits to consider:

Price Control
1. **Higher Sale Prices**: On average, "Buy It Now" items tend to sell for about 20-30% more compared to auctions.

Flexibility
2. **Best Offer Feature**: This function allows potential buyers to propose a price within a range you've set. You can automatically reject lowball offers and even set counteroffers, providing flexibility without constant monitoring.

Duration and Relisting

3. **Longer Listing Periods**: Buy It Now listings can be active for up to 30 days and can automatically be relisted if the item doesn't sell, saving you the hassle of manual relisting.

Making The Right Choice: Auction Or Buy It Now?

The "Auction" or "Buy It Now" decision is ultimately contextual. If your item is in high demand, scarce, and it's the right season, an auction could be exceptionally lucrative. On the other hand, if your item is relatively common, or the demand is low, "Buy It Now" provides a more stable and less risky platform to ensure you get a reasonable price.

So the next time you're about to list an item on eBay, weigh these factors carefully. Both options have their own unique set of advantages and downsides, but understanding these can help you maximize your profits and improve your overall selling experience.

HOW MUCH DOES IT COST TO LIST MY ITEMS?

Understanding the cost of listing items on eBay is crucial for sellers who aim to maximize their profits while maintaining competitive pricing. While eBay's fee structure can seem complicated at first glance, it becomes more straightforward once broken down.

Estimation Strategy

One approach to navigating eBay's fee system is to estimate the total cost as a percentage of your listing's selling price. Personally, I like to round this number up to approximately 20%. Though this is a high-end estimate—actual fees are likely closer to 15% —it provides a financial cushion. By overestimating, I can build the listing fees into my asking price and still have room for negotiation.

Basic Fee Structure

Let's delve into the fundamental fees that eBay charges its sellers:
Insertion Fees
These are the fees charged for simply placing your item on eBay's platform. Every seller gets a certain number of free listings per

month, depending on their account type. Beyond that limit, each additional listing incurs an insertion fee.

Additional Insertion Options
- **Bold Title ($4)**: This feature makes your listing title bold in search results, drawing more attention to it.
- **Subtitle ($1.50)**: A subtitle allows you to add extra descriptive text under your main title. It can be beneficial for highlighting unique selling points.
- **Show an Enlarged Photo in Search Results ($1)**: This feature enables your item's photo to appear larger in search results, thus attracting more eyeballs.

Promotion Fees

Promote Your Listing: eBay allows you to boost your listing's visibility through sponsored placements. You can set the percentage of the final sale price that you're willing to pay for this promotion. It's an auction-style process, meaning the higher the percentage, the more visibility your listing will get.

Auction Specific Fees

Auction Reserve Price: When conducting an auction, you can set a minimum threshold or "reserve" price for your item. If bidding doesn't reach this reserve, the item won't be sold. Setting a reserve price isn't free; eBay charges a fee for this service, which varies based on the reserve price you set.

Why Understanding Fees Is Crucial

Knowing eBay's fee structure inside out allows you to price your items strategically. You can build these fees into your selling price or consider them as a part of your operational costs. Either way, the clearer your understanding of these fees, the more accurately you can set your prices, and the more likely you are to make a satisfactory profit.

In conclusion, while eBay's fee structure may initially seem daunting, understanding the specifics can significantly impact your profitability. By budgeting for fees upfront and incorporating them into your listing prices, you create a buffer that allows you more flexibility and peace of mind as a seller.

HOW TO CRAFT AN EFFECTIVE EBAY LISTING

Creating an eBay listing is more than just an administrative task—it's an art form that can significantly influence your sales success. Now that you have identified what you're selling and received the necessary feedback, let's dive into the intricacies of crafting an irresistible eBay listing.

Crafting A Compelling Title

The title of your listing is essentially your first impression. A poorly-crafted title could mean potential buyers scroll right past your listing, but a compelling one will make them stop and pay attention. For example, if you're selling a gently-used grey Donna Karan cardigan in women's medium size, resist the urge to title your auction something mundane like

> "Womens Used Medium Donna Karan Cardigan – Grey."

Consider a more captivating alternative like:

> "STUNNING GREY DONNA KARAN CARDIGAN - Trendy,

Extra Soft & Comfortable. Women's Size M."

The second title not only grabs attention but also provides more information about the item's quality and comfort.

Tip: If your item has a model number or unique features, include those in the title. As for subtitles, I rarely use them. They often seem like an unnecessary expense, except for instances like selling bundles where it might be unavoidable.

Quality Over Quantity: Listing Photos

Photos can make or break your listing. Ensure your images are crisp, clear, and showcase the product from multiple angles. Utilize a clutter-free, solid-colored background that doesn't overshadow the item. Good lighting is also crucial to highlight the item's features and condition effectively.

Tip: Include pictures of model numbers, serial numbers, or other identifying details, because the truth is—many buyers simply don't read thoroughly.

Item Specifics: The Devil's In The Details

You might not have exhaustive product details at your fingertips, and that's okay. A quick Google search can usually provide the essential information needed to fill out the "Item Specifics" section. The more details you include, the more you protect yourself from uninformed buyers.

Crafting A Detailed Item Description

Your item description should be thorough and highlight all the benefits a potential buyer would get from winning the bid. Remember, online buyers can't physically interact with the product, making your description their only guide. Spell out every detail clearly, as you can't assume the buyer will read every part of your listing.

> **Anecdote**: *I once sold a set of 4 single tires. So, I posted the listing Qty 4 Bridgestone tires 99% tread life remaining. In the specifications I specified that the listing was for a quantity of one tire with a total quantity of four available for sale. in the auction description I specified that the auction is for "four individual tires". In the photos I showed all four tires and tread.*
>
> *These tires were just taking up room in my garage, so I priced them on the lower end at $125 + shipping. I thought I was sweet. I'd clearly explained in multiple places that I am selling each tire individually and not as a set. But what do you think happened? Not 1, not 2, not 3 but ALL 4 buyers thought they were getting a set of 4 darn near brand new tires, Bridgestone no less, for $125 because they saw 4 tires in the pictures.*
>
> *Did they read the item specifies? NO! Did they read the description? NO! Back Buyer treated my listing as if it was a children picture back. They completely ignored the words and only looked at the photos.*

To avoid such misunderstandings, craft your description so it leaves no room for interpretation. Assume your buyers won't read everything and make your point redundantly clear.

Taking the extra time to craft an effective eBay listing can save you from misunderstandings, reduce returns, and help ensure a successful sale. In the next book, we'll explore instances where buyer behavior could work to your advantage—but for now, make your listings as detailed as possible to appeal to the broadest audience.

What Should I Not Include In My Auction Description?

Navigating the fine line between transparency and oversharing in your auction description is crucial for effective selling on eBay. The goal is to offer just the right amount of information—enough to instill trust and encourage a purchase, but not so much that it scares potential buyers away. Let's explore how to strike this balance.

The Pitfalls Of Oversharing

For instance, imagine you're selling a used iPhone 11 with minor screen scratches and other negligible issues. While you may be tempted to over-disclose every little detail, doing so could deter potential buyers.

Oversharing Example:
"Up for sale is a used iPhone 11. The screen has 5 scratches on the screen. There are 6 areas of very slight discoloration. The left side of the apple logo on the back of the phone is faded. I have had a problem with the phone freezing about 3 times over the last 2 years. I have reported it to Apple each time. The charging cord is not included. My daughter lost it last year or I would have included it."

This description, although honest, may dissuade buyers more than it builds trust. It's essential to remember that buyers are generally aware that used items won't be in brand-new condition. Your focus should be on creating a balanced portrayal.

Balanced Description Example:
"This auction is for a gently used iPhone 11. There are some minor scratches on the screen, but scratches are not deep and have never stopped me from playing Candy Crush. In fact, the scratches

cannot even be seen when backlight is on. There are some normal signs of wear, but phone functions as intended. Charging Cord not included but it does come with original box. Please see all photos and ask questions prior to bidding. Thanks!"

This reimagined description provides a fair and honest account while emphasizing the product's positive aspects. It covers the item's flaws but does so in a way that doesn't overshadow its functionality and overall value.

Honesty Is Non-Negotiable

It's imperative to clarify that avoiding oversharing does not equate to being dishonest. Transparency is key to building a long-term, sustainable business on eBay. Misrepresenting an item can lead to customer complaints, returns, and even the closure of your eBay account. The headaches associated with handling disputes far outweigh any short-term gains from a quick sale based on a misleading description.

Tips For Crafting An Ideal Description:

- **Be Honest, but Concise**: Clearly disclose any defects or damage, but don't dwell on them.
- **Highlight Positive Features**: Make sure to point out what makes the item valuable or desirable.
- **Include Necessary Details**: Specify what is and isn't included in the sale, such as accessories or original packaging.
- **Encourage Questions**: Inviting prospective buyers to ask questions can clear up any ambiguities and foster trust.

In summary, while crafting your auction description, be honest, smart, and strategic. By doing so, you can maximize your item's appeal without compromising on integrity, ultimately driving higher bids and more successful sales.

MASTERING THE ART OF SHIPPING ON EBAY: A COMPREHENSIVE GUIDE

Shipping is one of the most crucial aspects of selling on eBay, often making the difference between a satisfied customer and a less-than-stellar review. With the right shipping strategies, not only will you provide excellent customer service, but eBay will also reward you with better visibility and potentially more sales.

Importance Of Customer Service In Shipping

Excellent customer service should be your guiding principle when setting up your shipping policy. eBay encourages this by incentivizing sellers to offer quick handling times and accepting returns. Remember, one-day handling time doesn't mean one-day shipping; it refers to the time it takes you to process the order.

Handling Time And Tracking Numbers

Be proactive in creating shipping labels and uploading tracking numbers as eBay's handling time clock stops ticking once the tracking details are uploaded. However, avoid extensive delays between uploading the tracking information and actually shipping the item. eBay has delivery window guidelines, and it's in your best interest to adhere to them.

Deciphering The Right Shipping Charges

Determining the appropriate amount to charge for shipping can be a perplexing task. A helpful strategy is to observe what other sellers are charging for shipping similar items. Don't rely solely on guesstimates; they can often lead to inaccurate shipping costs, affecting your profit margins.

The Abcs Of Setting Up Shipping Options

Here are the various shipping methods you can consider:
1. **Local Pickup Only**: Best for bulky or fragile items that can't be shipped conveniently.
2. **Flat Rate Shipping**: This involves charging a fixed fee regardless of the customer's location.
3. **Calculated Shipping**: eBay calculates the shipping cost based on the item's weight and dimensions.

Expert Tip: Avoid eBay's Calculated Shipping
As a seasoned eBay seller, I strongly discourage using eBay's calculated shipping feature—it is notoriously inaccurate.

Why Flat Rate Shipping Is King

I personally recommend flat-rate shipping. It's hassle-free, and the necessary supplies are often available for free. Plus, knowing your shipping costs upfront allows you to add a small handling fee. The padded flat rate envelope from USPS is especially versatile; you can order them directly from the USPS website and they're perfect for a wide range of items from cosmetics to footwear.

Weight And Carrier Considerations

For packages under 10 lbs or with dimensions smaller than 12 inches, USPS is usually the most cost-effective option. For larger or heavier items, consider using UPS or FedEx.

Unlock Savings With A Fedex Business Account

Consider setting up a FedEx Business Account to save between 10-25% on shipping costs. Although the account doesn't require official business documentation, you'll need to provide credit card details. This account allows you to print your own labels, and any discrepancies in weight or dimensions are adjusted later. I recommend erring on the side of caution when estimating weight and dimensions to avoid overcharges.

Your shipping policy can greatly affect your customer service ratings and, in turn, your overall eBay success. Make informed decisions based on your product type, customer base, and preferred carriers. By doing so, you can streamline your shipping process, save money, and improve customer satisfaction.

NAVIGATING THE COMPLEXITIES OF GETTING PAID ON EBAY

The eBay marketplace has undergone significant changes over the years, particularly in how sellers receive payments for their goods. The transition from allowing sellers to use various payment processors like PayPal to eBay's own managed payments system has been, to put it mildly, a bumpy ride for many. Here's a comprehensive guide to understanding this payment system, its challenges, and how best to navigate it.

The Basics Of Ebay Managed Payments

In theory, eBay's managed payments system aims to be a one-stop solution for all transaction processes. Customers can pay using their preferred methods, such as credit cards or PayPal, and the money initially goes into your eBay account. eBay then deducts any applicable fees before depositing the net amount into your bank account.

Scheduled Deposits

Unlike some other platforms that offer instant transfers, eBay's managed payments are usually scheduled. You can opt for daily or weekly deposits, but it's essential to note that even daily deposits can take up to 2-3 business days to appear in your bank account.

Challenges With Ebay Managed Payments

Transparency Issues with Fees
One of the most significant challenges that sellers face is the lack of transparency around fees. eBay deducts various fees, such as final value fees and potential promotional fees, but these are often not clearly itemized or deducted in a systematic manner. This opacity can make it incredibly difficult to determine your actual profit margins.

Delayed Payments
With eBay managing the payments, many sellers have experienced delays in receiving their funds, especially when compared to third-party payment processors. This delay can affect your cash flow and your ability to reinvest quickly into new inventory.

Currency Conversion and International Sales
For those who sell internationally, the managed payments system complicates matters further. Currency conversion fees can be added, and these are yet another cost you need to account for when calculating your potential profits.

Proactive Strategies For Navigating Ebay Payments

1. **Detailed Record-Keeping**: Maintain a thorough record of all transactions, including the selling price, shipping fees, and any additional charges. This way, you can cross-reference these with the amounts eventually deposited into your bank account.
2. **Use Accounting Software**: Invest in specialized accounting software tailored for online sellers, which can automate the

process of tracking eBay fees and other costs.
3. **Cash Flow Management**: Given the delays in payments, you'll need a robust cash flow management strategy to ensure that you can continue to operate efficiently. Plan for these delays in your budget.
4. **Seek Professional Advice**: If you're selling on eBay as a full-time business, it may be worth consulting with a financial advisor who specializes in e-commerce.
5. **Community Support**: Never underestimate the power of community. Other sellers can offer invaluable advice, especially when dealing with a system as confusing as eBay's. Online forums, webinars, and community guides can be a goldmine of information.

In conclusion, eBay's managed payments system can be cumbersome and unclear, but it's not insurmountable. With a proactive approach, detailed record-keeping, and a willingness to adapt to changing circumstances, you can navigate this system to your advantage. Be prepared for challenges, but also remember: knowledge is power. The more you understand the intricacies of eBay's payment process, the better positioned you'll be to succeed.

THE ULTIMATE GUIDE TO CUSTOMER SERVICE ON EBAY

In the realm of online selling, customer service isn't just an added benefit; it's a cornerstone of your entire business. As most eBay sellers know, customer feedback isn't just numbers or stars—it's your business's reputation. Even a minor blip of negative reviews can have a ripple effect on your earnings and future sales. Therefore, it's paramount that your customer service doesn't just meet but exceeds expectations. Here's a more detailed guide on how to make that happen:

The Importance Of Seamless Communication

Immediate Post-Purchase Engagement
Once a transaction is complete, make the first move by reaching out to thank the buyer for their business. It's not just courteous but also opens the door to addressing any queries or concerns they may have before you ship the item.

Providing Real-Time Updates
Transparency is crucial. Make sure to upload tracking numbers promptly. This proactive approach reassures the buyer and enhances their shopping experience.

Post-Delivery Follow-up
It's good business practice to confirm that the customer has received their order and is satisfied with it. This second thank-you note serves as another touchpoint, emphasizing your focus on customer satisfaction. Additionally, it provides a gentle avenue to request feedback.

Promptness in Addressing Concerns
Never leave emails or queries unanswered for long. Quick and efficient communication makes customers feel valued and heard. This kind of respect often converts into positive reviews and, more importantly, repeat business.

Adding A Personal Touch

Handwritten Notes
The world has gone digital, but the impact of a handwritten thank-you note is still unparalleled. It makes the customer feel individually valued and appreciated, which increases the chances of them becoming a repeat buyer.

Surprise Inclusions
Consider adding small, cost-effective freebies relevant to the purchased item. This unexpected touch often delights customers, increasing the likelihood of positive reviews.

Resolving Disputes Effectively And Efficiently

Open Dialogue
If a customer isn't satisfied with their purchase, always attempt to resolve the issue privately before it escalates to eBay's customer service. An open and honest dialogue can often solve problems more efficiently and amicably.

The Art of Compromise
Contrary to the saying, the customer isn't always right. However, finding a compromise that leaves both parties somewhat satisfied is the hallmark of excellent customer service. This might involve partial refunds, discounts on future purchases, or other solutions that preserve your relationship with the customer without compromising your profitability.

Upcoming Topics for Advanced Sellers
This chapter provides a foundational understanding of customer service best practices. For a more in-depth exploration of other facets of eBay selling—such as setting up a store, navigating disputes, and understanding technical support and account regulations—stay tuned for Volume 2 of this guide.

By embracing these customer service best practices, you'll not only maintain an impressive feedback profile but also create a sustainable eBay business built on a foundation of trust, value, and customer loyalty.

THE EBAY BUYER'S BIBLE: EVERYTHING YOU NEED TO KNOW TO BUY SMART AND SAVE MONEY

While Amazon might be the contemporary giant of online retail, eBay remains an unparalleled universe of eclectic items and unbeatable bargains. Even though eBay's reputation has been blemished by instances of scams and unreliable sellers, the platform is rich with opportunities—featuring over 1 billion listings at any given moment. I've personally unearthed incredible finds on eBay, subsequently relisting them to turn a neat profit.

Unveiling the eBay Marketplace: The Good and The Bad
Before diving into our expert tips for a fruitful eBay experience, it's worth acknowledging the platform's mixed reputation. Yes, there are sellers who might not know the ropes or even try to scam you. But conversely, there are also countless reputable sellers and hidden gems waiting to be discovered. Your success on eBay is largely contingent on your approach and the strategies you employ.

Expert Tips For A Smooth Ebay Shopping Experience

1. Maximize the Auction Experience: The Sniping Strategy
Auctions offer not just the thrill of bidding but also a legitimate avenue for snagging eye-popping deals. Specifically target auctions that are set to end at less popular hours, like late at night or early in the morning. Employ the sniping technique, which involves placing your highest acceptable bid mere seconds before the auction ends, thereby reducing the chance for others to counter-bid.

Why Does Sniping Work?

Many eBay auctions gather the most action during the final moments. By entering the fray at the last possible second, you minimize the time available for someone else to place a higher bid, thus increasing your chances of walking away the winner.

2. The "Buy It Now" and "Best Offer" Combo
If your auction hunting comes up short, look for items listed under "Buy It Now" that also allow a "Best Offer." This feature provides a three-attempt window to negotiate the price. Leverage this opportunity to ask for bundled items, discounted shipping, or any other perks that could add value to your purchase.

Creative Negotiating Tactics

Don't limit your offers to mere price reductions. Consider proposing a package deal of multiple items from the same seller or even asking for an expedited shipping option at no additional cost.

3. Informed Bidding: The Importance of Clarity
Read every word of the listing description, and scrutinize

all available specifications. When in doubt, don't hesitate to communicate directly with the seller to clarify any uncertainties. Aim to get any verbal promises in writing as evidence should the need for a dispute arise.

Document Everything

Keep a record of all correspondence with the seller. If you end up receiving an item that doesn't match its description, this documentation will be invaluable for filing a dispute with eBay.

4. Photos Tell a Story: Look for Authenticity

Stock images are professionally done, but they often don't represent the actual condition of the item you're considering. Always prioritize listings that include real, high-quality photos. If these aren't available, contact the seller to request additional pictures.

5. Seller Feedback: A Treasure Trove of Insight

Feedback ratings are more than just numbers; they're a reflection of a seller's history on eBay. Do some investigative work—ignore overly generic or suspiciously positive feedback and focus on reviews that detail specific experiences.

Read Between the Lines

Even negative feedback can be informative. Did the seller attempt to resolve the issue? Was it a one-time oversight or part of a pattern? Use this information to make a more educated decision about the seller.

6. Know Your Rights: eBay's Buyer Protection Policy

Educate yourself thoroughly on eBay's Buyer Protection Policy. Be aware that any attempt to use feedback as a bargaining tool is prohibited and could jeopardize your buyer protection rights.

Bookmark the Policy Page

Keep eBay's protection policy page handy for quick reference. The better you understand your rights, the more effectively you can act if something goes wrong.

7. Safeguard Your Transactions: Stay Within eBay's Boundaries
Engaging in transactions outside of eBay exposes you to all sorts of risks, from scams to potential account suspension. Always keep your dealings within the platform to benefit from eBay's protection measures.

8. Stack Your Savings: Cashback Apps and More
Integrate cashback apps like Ebates and CouponCabin into your eBay shopping for an extra layer of discounts. It's a straightforward way to make your dollars stretch further.

9. Secure Payment Methods: Your Financial Safety Net
Prioritize payment methods that offer robust buyer protection, like PayPal or established credit card companies. American Express is particularly recommended due to its comprehensive buyer safeguards.

10. International Purchases: A Cautionary Tale
Buying internationally can unearth unique items but comes with its set of challenges, such as longer shipping times and the possibility of additional duties and taxes. Always clarify who is responsible for any extra fees before committing to a purchase.

A Closing Note: Building Your Ebay Skillset

Navigating eBay is a skill—one that requires a blend of research, timing, and judicious decision-making. By following this comprehensive guide, you equip yourself with the know-how to score incredible deals while sidestepping the potential pitfalls that can snare unwary buyers. With the right strategies, eBay becomes not just a shopping platform but a venue for exciting discoveries and valuable acquisitions. Happy treasure hunting!

FRAZIER CUNNINGHAM

TAKING FLIGHT: YOUR EBAY JOURNEY AHEAD

Congratulations and Well Done!

You've done it! You've mastered the art of buying and selling on eBay. The path to eBay success isn't reserved for geniuses; it's paved with dedication and fueled by passion. So as you embark on this exciting venture, remember that your achievement is bound only by your commitment and enthusiasm.

Strategic Planning

Be clear and realistic about what you aim to achieve. Crafting a well-thought-out business plan is not just a good idea—it's a necessity. Stick to your plan rigorously but be open to adaptations as the market evolves.

Building Trust and Protecting Interests

Transparency and honesty go a long way in establishing customer loyalty. However, as you build these customer relationships, also focus on securing your interests as a seller. Familiarize yourself with eBay's policies and safeguards, so you can trade confidently and securely.

Staying Ahead of the Game

Knowledge is power. Stay updated on market trends, hot-selling items, and customer preferences. Keep an eye out for new suppliers and potential business partnerships that align with your goals and could benefit your growth.

Price Smartly

Remember, it's not just about staying competitive—it's also about sustaining your business. Make sure your pricing strategy allows for healthy profit margins. Your growth depends on your ability to reinvest in your business, so plan your pricing accordingly.

Navigating eBay's Regulatory Landscape

eBay operates under a set of rules designed to maintain a fair marketplace for both buyers and sellers. Acquaint yourself thoroughly with these regulations and learn to leverage them to your advantage. Doing so not only helps you avoid pitfalls but can also provide unexpected opportunities to grow your business.

The Power Is in Your Hands

Ultimately, the trajectory of your eBay business is entirely within your control. With a combination of dedication, strategic planning, and a continual pursuit of knowledge, there's no limit to what you can achieve.

Your journey on eBay is yours to command. Go out there and conquer the marketplace—your future awaits!

ABOUT THE AUTHOR

Frazier Cunningham Iii

Frazier Cunningham III is not just an entrepreneur; he's a serial entrepreneur who has an impressive track record of building multiple seven-figure businesses on eBay. His entrepreneurial journey began at the age of 18 when he founded his own furniture store in Detroit, laying the foundation for a career steeped in ingenuity and business acumen.

Through decades in the retail industry, Frazier has honed the skills necessary to excel in a competitive market. He possesses an in-depth understanding of sourcing, marketing, and promoting both new and used items. His years of hands-on experience have also endowed him with the keen ability to foster and develop invaluable relationships with online selling platforms, transforming them into robust channels for business growth.

But Frazier's talents don't stop at entrepreneurship. He is also a visionary inventor, holding multiple patents that bear testimony to his creative thinking and commitment to innovation. His ingenuity often blends seamlessly with his entrepreneurial ventures, providing him a unique edge in a market that is constantly evolving.

Frazier's business ethos is rooted in dedication, strategic planning, and an unquenchable thirst for knowledge—qualities that have been instrumental in his remarkable success.

Away from the hustle and bustle of the business world, Frazier is a dedicated family man. He resides in Michigan with his wife and family, where he enjoys the fruits of his labor but never loses sight of the next big opportunity.

With an incredible career that spans decades and industries, Frazier Cunningham III stands as a living testament to what is possible with the right mix of dedication, intelligence, and courage. He continues to be an inspiration to aspiring entrepreneurs, embodying the essence of American business spirit.